DANTE'S DIVINE COMEDY

Illuminated Manuscripts

DANTE'S DIVINE COMEDY

15th – Century Manuscript

Commentaries on the Miniatures by
Prof. Sergio Samek-Ludovici

Narration by
Nino Ravenna

Translated by
Peter J. Tallon

Crescent Books
Distributed by Crown Publishers, Inc.

Venice, Biblioteca Nazionale Marciana, Cod. It. IX, 276 (=6902).
Photos by Carlo Aschieri.

We wish to thank Dr Gian Albino Ravalli Modoni, Director of the Biblioteca
Nazionale Marciana, for his kind and valuable assistance.

Durante Alighieri, known by the nickname of Dante, was born in Florence on May 8, 1265 and died in Ravenna on September 14, 1321. He belonged to a noble family and was the great-grandson of Cacciaguida Elizei, who had married a young woman of the Alighieris or Aldighieris of Ferrara, and whose children adopted the coat of arms and the name. Cacciaguida followed Emperor Conrad III to the crusades and was killed at a battle in Syria in 1147. (In Cantos XV, XVI and XVII of *Paradise,* Cacciaguida is supposed to recount his adventures to Dante, while at the same time providing an interesting description of Florence and its life before the great split between Guelphs and Ghibellines devastated the town).

Aldighiero Alighieri, Dante's father, died while his son was still small, but his mother, Bella, whose maiden name was unknown, took care to give him a good education and sent him to the famous Bruno Latini, a statesman who was both a scientist and a poet. It was about this time that Dante met Guido Cavalcanti with whom he formed a friendship that was to last until Guido's death. Guido was much older than his friend and seems to have played a significant part in Dante's education. It is claimed that Dante studied in Bologna, although there is no absolute proof of this. His writings show that his studies covered most fields and that he was acquainted with all branches of contemporary knowledge.

According to what he says himself, his life was rather reprobate until he met Beatrice Portinari, from one of the most illustrious Florentine families. He immediately felt for her a love that was deep, but apparently Platonic, and caused him to turn to a better way of living. Several biographers claim that this love dated from Dante's earliest years, and that it was around the age of nine that he felt the first pangs. This is a fact that Dante himself seems to contradict in his poem *Vita Nuova,* written around 1290, roughly about the time of his beloved's death. Around 1287, she had married Simone Bardi, without the marriage affecting the purely religious aspect of Dante's love for her. In *Vita Nuova* he talks of this love as an ideal thing and above all underlines the change it brought about in him. Indeed he cherished the memory of Beatrice until his dying day and immortalized her in his poems.

At the time when Dante reached adulthood, the Guelphs reigned in Florence, from where the Ghibellines had been driven several years before with the help of the Pope and Charles of Anjou, king of Naples. On the other hand, the Glibellines ruled in Arezzo, where the bishop was their leader, and had thrown out the Guelphs. The latter called for the help of their brothers in Florence and war soon broke out. It was ended in June 1289 by the battle of Campoldino, where the Arezzo Ghibellines were defeated, and where their bishop, who marched at their head, was killed. Dante took part in the battle, showing great courage, and helped his townsmen to win.

It was shortly after his return to Florence that, on his parents' insistence, he married Gemma Donati, from a powerful Guelph family. It was also about this time that he began to look for fame and civil employment.

At that time the citizens of Florence were divided into three classes: the *grandi,* or ancient families, many of whom still had lordly manors near Florence, with all the privileges of feudal law, although within the city these were refused; the *popolani grassi,* or rich citizens, whose wealth came mostly from trade and of whom many were richer than the aristocracy; finally, the *piccioli,* or plebeians, workers, craftsmen, etc. The two latter classes were tired of the troubles caused by the factions and were led by men of sound judgment among whom was the historian Dino Compagni, the best guide to be found for a description of the chaotic history of Florence at that period. In 1282, a law was passed dividing citizens into a certain number of corporations, according to job or function. Initially, there were 14 of these corporations but eventually their number grew to 21. The higher corporations, or *arti maggiori,* elected six priors or aldermen, who were also called *i signori* and who were changed every six months. No one could present himself for the position of prior unless he was on the register of one of these corporations. Dante was ambitious to be a magistrate, to which his birth and knowledge, which was already widely recognized, entitled him to aspire. He put his name on the register of doctors and apothecaries, which were in the sixth class, but he never exercised either of these professions.

The priors' establishment was unable to prevent Florence from being upset by the factions, as the magistrates them-selves were influenced by their own friendships, as well as by pressure from the more influential aristocrats. To counteract this state of affairs, the popular party, under the leadership of its chief, Giano della Bella, elected a new magistrate in 1293 called *gonfaloniere di giustizza,* who was mandated to re-establish order, to see that justice was done for all; for this he was provided with a guard of 1,000 soldiers. At the same time the party excluded the 33 *grandi* or aristocratic families from all public offices. But by the next year a conspiracy had overthrown Giano della Bella and his supporters, and civil strife began again.

Two powerful families, the Donati and the Cerchi, led the two main factions and the streets of Florence ran with blood every day. However, both these families belonged to the Guelph party, but the Cerchi were suspected of having leanings towards the Ghibelline side as they were less active in their persecution of the latter, and several of them were friends of the exiled Giano della Bella. The Donati were supported by Pope Boniface VIII, who saw them as the most determined leaders of the Guelph party. At the same period, the town of Pistoia was also split into two factions, the Blacks and the Whites, who chose Florence to be their judge; some of the most headstrong members of both parties came to Florence as refugees, where the Whites took the Cerchi side and the Blacks the Donati. The colors soon came to be used for the Florentine factions. Both, as noted, belonged to the Guelph party, but the Whites were soon to join the Ghibellines, and historians were nearly always to mix up their names.

Dante was a Guelph, but became a relative of the Donatis

by marriage; but his personal relationships, and probably a feeling of fairness, drew him to the Ghibellines, who at the beginning seemed to be less tyrannical and less violent than their adversaries, and were, in fact, the underdog. Raised to the office of prior in the month of June 1300, Dante proposed and enacted a law which exiled the leaders of both parties outside the territory of the Republic: the Whites were sent to Sarzana and the Blacks to Castello della Piave. However, some of the Whites, among them Guido Cavalcanti, lost no time in returning to Florence, and Dante was accused of having helped them return, mainly because of his close friendship with Guido.

In January 1302 he was sentenced to two years of exile, a fine of 8,000 florins and, if he failed to pay the fine, to have his goods confiscated. This was not sufficient: a second sentence, passed in March of the same year, condemned him, as well as several others, to be burned alive being guilty of embezzlement, and usury. The sentence, written in bad Latin, claims that he was condemned on public evidence, *fama publica,* which of course was provided by his enemies.

So started Dante's painful wanderings in exile. He split completely from the Guelphs and sought to push the Italian Ghibellines against his enemies and against the country's oppressors. Shortly afterwards he was to be found in Verona, which at that time was governed by the Della Scala family, one the most powerful in the Ghibelline party; but he soon left this town to come back to Tuscany, where the Whites and the Ghibellines, united in revenge, were assembling their forces near Arezzo.

In 1306 Dante went to Padua and the next year was in the court of the Malaspina, the lords of Lunigiana; shortly after, he was wandering in the valleys of Casentino and in the mountains near Arezzo. It is said that about this time he made a trip to Paris, although it seems that if he ever went there, then it was in or after 1313, following the death of Henry VII, the Emperor. Several writers doubt that he ever visited the French capital although (in *Paradise,* Canto X) he sang the praises of a certain Sigier, a professor a the university in that city, and whose street address he even gives.

It was at about this period that he attempted to obtain his recall from exile, sending a pathetic letter to his countrymen, which began with these words: "Oh my people, what have I done to you?" But the attempt was without success; the Adimari family, who had been given possession of the poet's goods, opposed his return; he returned the compliment by imprecating them in his best way *(Paradise,* Canto XVI).

Dante had to take refuge in Verona, at Cane della Scala's court. This appears to have been from 1308 to 1310. Cane provided the most generous hospitality to Ghibelline émigrés; but Dante, independent by nature and embittered by adversity, could not bring himself to endure the flattery of court or the scurrility of courtiers. It is said that he was made to suffer and was humiliated by the entourage of the ruler of Verona. In a most touching way, he described the exile's fate in a well-know passage from his great poem:

Tu proverai si come sà di sale
Lo pane altrui, e com'è duro calle
La scendere, e'l salir per l'altrui scalle.
(Paradise, canto XVII)

"You'll find out how rancid another man's bread is, and

how difficult it is to climb or go down another man's staircase." However, it seems that he never lost Cane della Scale's protection, for, in the lines of his poem that immediately precede the ones above, he sings the praises of this prince of Verona. There is even an affectionate letter still in existence probably dating from the last years of his life, in which he dedicates the last part of *Paradise* to Cane, and explains the subject to him.

He establishes a difference between the literal and the allegorical meaning of his verse, and noted that his poem could be called *Polysensuum,* or of many meanings. He then states the full title of the work: *Incipit Comoedia Dantis Alighieri, Florentini natione non moribus;* but the title of the part sent to Cane is: *Incipit cantica tertia Comoedia Dantie, quoe dicitur Paradisus.* This tends to demonstrate that Cane did not know the rest of the poem; in fact, it is probable that the poet never sent the full work to anybody during his life, as he could not find shelter anywhere.

Around 1316 an opportunity to return to his homeland was offered to the poet, but under such conditions that he could not make his mind up to accept it. One of his friends, probably a priest, as Dante calls him father in his letters, wrote to him that it would be easy to come back to Florence if he were to admit his guilt and ask for forgiveness for his sins *(crimes?)* of the past. Dante's character shows up in his reply: "No, father, this is not the way that will bring me back to my country; but I will come back quickly if you, or any other, open a door to me that does not affect Dante's honor or glory. But if the only way back to Florence is the one you offer me, then I will never return. After all, the sun and the stars shine elsewhere too. Can I not search and find truth under other skies, without ruining my glory, without making myself infamous to the people of Florence? Dante, I hope, will never go without bread."

The last years of exile, mainly 1316 to 1318, were perhaps more bitter for the poet than the first, as he wandered all over, to the Tyrol, Friule and Gubbio. In 1319, he appeared at the court of Guido da Polenta, lord of Ravenna, who received him with the greatest honor and at whose court he probably stayed until his death. He was buried in the Church of the Minor Friars of Saint Francis. Guido, who was forced by the fortunes of war to leave the town soon after, only had the time to place a simple marble stone on his tomb, without any inscription. Bernado Bembo, a senator of Venice and magistrate of Ravenna, had an impressive tomb built in 1483, which was repaired in 1692 by Cardinal Corsi of Florence, and completely rebuilt on its present site in 1780.

The Florentines tried on many occasions to bring back the mortal remains their of greatest citizen, whom they had banned and dismissed without pity; all their efforts failed and Ravenna refused to give up such a precious possession.

There is no authentic portrait of the Italian Homer; Boccaccio alone passed down information about him that can be considered reliable, as it was taken from the relations and friends of the exiled poets. His description was used by many artists in drawing the writer of the *Divine Comedy*. Because of this there is a kind of family resemblance in all the portraits of Dante; the same features can be found in all of them. Some portraits show Dante with a long face, aquiline nose, large eyes, jutting lower lip, dark features, beard and black hair that is thick and curly, kindly yet melancholy and pensive air. Boccaccio tells us that he was of medium height, that his gait was noble and serious; that in all his relationships he was modest and reserved, rarely speaking, but that, when he did so it was with irresistible eloquence. He liked the company of women and was gay with them. His way of life was simple, although he liked to dress well.

His genius embraced every science; from his youth he studied art and music and, gifted in singing, he liked to sing during the rare moments of peace and joy that came his way during his life. Later, he took up natural sciences and metaphysics, studied the languages of southern Europe and even took up Greek, Hebrew and Arabic, which he gained a working knowledge of. The proof can be found in his work that he had a profound understanding of the factions and secret doctrines of the Church.

It was about 1300 that Dante started to write the *Divine Comedy*, to which he was to devote 18 years of his life. It is in fact a trilogy, a play in three acts: *Hell, Purgatory,* and *Paradise*. Each of the three parts were called *Canticles* in the original language and were subdivided into short cantos of 130 to 140 verses each; the cantos total 100 in number. At the end of each canticle, the poet used the word *stelle* —stars— to rhyme with the last verse of the last stanza. Why he did this remains a mystery.

The first canto of *Hell* is the introduction to the whole work. Dante supposes that he is "midway along the path of life", at the entrance to a dark forest, the simple reminder of which fills him with anguish. He tries to go ahead, but horrible beasts block his way. It is at this moment that Virgil appears from the shadows and proposes to guide him. Dante accepts and with the Latin poet undertakes his long journey through the world of shades. Virgil warns him that he will only accompany him through Hell and Purgatory, and that in Paradise, another guide, Beatrice, will lead him through those worlds, the threshold of which no pagan can cross. Then begins the Florentine's famous journey through the world of the damned and the souls in torment.

This is the most frightening and most famous part of the poem; the singular variety of punishments, the speed with

which Dante presents the most famous damned of history and describes in an unforgettable way the grimacing faces, the grace of certain episodes among so much horror, are all witness to an unrivalled imagination. Three descriptions stand out against such a dark background: the adventure of Francesca of Rimini and of Paola, the death of Hugolino and of Manfred. From the center of the Earth, where Hell is located, Dante climbs to the planets, from there to the stars, and even beyond that.

Thanks to Lucifer's huge size and the fact that he raises Mount Purgatory as high as the planets, the poet enters a new kingdom which, like Hell, is divided, into circuits and circles, arranged in an admirable pattern. Earthly Paradise is at the summit of this mountain. In Purgatory, Dante sees sights of suffering and punishment, but these are only temporary penances. The poet hesitates to cross a path of flame, but Virgil says to him: "There is only this wall between you and Beatrice." On hearing these words, Dante throws himself into the middle of the flames.

Once in the Earthly Paradise, the two poets see Beatrice appear in the middle of a magnificent vision: a divine forest, rushes blown by gentle breezes, the melodious singing of birds, green all around, and ink-black shadows. It is the sort of thing that a man from the dry south would like to find. Led by a woman singing a delightful melody, and her path strewn with flowers, Beatrice appears in her glory. This amorous vision is one of the most picturesque scenes, but it also apocalyptic.

Purified after his trials, the poets ascends into heaven at such speed that *neither tongue nor pen could follow*. This supreme Paradise is made up of ten Circles or Heavens; Earth is held immobile at the centre of the universe. Dante first passes the seven planets: the Moon, Mercury, Venus, the Sun, Mars, Jupiter and Saturn, then enters the eighth globe, then the Empyrean. Each of these globes is inhabited by souls and spirits. Moving from heaven to heaven, the poet is accompanied by Beatrice, whose smile encourages him to tread in her luminous footsteps. In the various spheres, he sees or distributes according to their merits and perfections those who were more or less without sin and who enjoy a

beatitude or splendor in accordance with their earthly existence.

In the eighth sphere Dante admires our own globe which appears so miserable to him that he smiles in pity. Beatrice reminds him of the highest contemplation: "There, she cries, is the procession surrounding Christ triumphant!" But the poet cannot bear the brilliance of this scene. In the ninth sphere, thanks to Beatrice's virtue, Dante is allowed to witness an ecstatic contemplation. He is in the presence of the divine essence, which is veiled by three hierarchies of angels which surround it. Beatrice explains to her friend the nature of the Empyrean and the way that the firmament works. Beatrice's beauty is transfigured to supreme perfection. Dante, shorn of all human desires, sees the sould of the blessed filling a huge ampitheatre, the rows of which spread ever wider and wider. Beatrice has taken her seat of glory; from her lofty new position she smiles to Dante then turns towards him who is the source of eternal light. These, in brief, are the marvels of Dante's trilogy.

Dante called his poem *Comedy; Divine* was added after his death. He himself revealed the reasons which made him choose the name: "Comedy is a kind of poetic composition that is different from all others. It differs from tragedy, because tragedy is beautiful and peaceful at the beginning, horrible at the end. Comedy, on the other hand, starts off badly, but has a happy ending, as can be seen in Terence's plays. Since then some poets have traditionally wished, in the form of a friendly greeting, a *tragic beginning and a comic ending*. The two species also differ in language. That of tragedy is high-flown and sublime; that of comedy is relaxed and simple, as Horace sought in his poetry. This is why the work is called *Comedy*. If you look at the subject, it is horrible and hideous at first: it is hell; and at the end it is happy desirable and graceful: it is paradise. If you look at the language, it is in a relaxed and simple style, as it is the common language which women use."

A letter by one of his contemporaries, Hilary, who was superior in a monastery where the poet took refuge to avoid banishment, tells us, moreover, that Dante had been on the point of sacrificing the vernacular, which his works did so much to enhance, to Latin, which was at the time the only language favored in the schools; he had even started the work with:

Ultima regna canam fluido contermina mundo,
Spiritibus quoe late patent, quoe proemia solvunt
Pro meritis quicumque suis!

If he had not have changed his mind, the world would have lost a masterpiece.

The *Divine Comedy* has given rise to a huge number of commentaries, historical works, prose and verse translations in virtually all languages. From the 15th century onwards, professorial chairs were established at Italian universities with a view to explaining the great Dantean epic—and not only in literature and scholastic philosophy, but also in law; indeed it has been said of Dante, who was thought to know everything—*Dantes nullius dogmatis expers*—that the categories into which he divided crimes and offenses were so accurate that modern penal thinking is still based on them.

Dante cannot be reasonably compared to any poet before or after him. He is quite original. The huge amount of

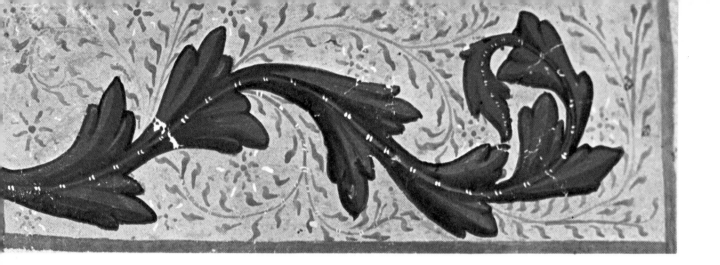

knowledge that he acquired never really affected his genius. An Italian critic said: "Dante invented a new type of poetry; he is original both in the outline and the detail of his work; he created ideas and language which expressed them." What sets Dante apart from other epic poets, either ancient or modern, is the singular novelty of his subject. He left aside heroes and fables, battles and swordfighting and offered a more useful and grandiose vehicle than the combats and the marvels of mythology. It is of no importance that the legend of Orpheus and Ulysses' descent to the underworld were the inspiration for his work. What gives *Divine Comedy* its unique character is the profound morality of the poem, its infinite scope, its harsh and vigorous censuring of the morals of the world, the satire, the reproval of civil war, the contrast between contemporary history and the view of another world, which showed up excess and bad deeds, and the striking visions that are spread throughout the work.

This titanic work, which, according to the French writer Lamennais, "summarized the whole Middle Ages before it sank into the depths of time. Something gloomy surrounds the whole fantastic apparition. There are shouts of despair, tears, unfathomable melancholy, and even joy is full of sadness; one feels as if one is at a funeral, standing by a coffin in an old cathedral draped in mourning. And yet a breath of life, a breath that revives what is dead under a more perfect shape, blows under the beams and across the nave of the great building, where, like the breast of a woman near to giving birth, a hidden trembling can be detected. The poem is both a tomb and a cradle: the magnificent tomb of a departing world, the cradle of a world about to emerge; a

portico between two temples, the temple of the past leaving its ideas, beliefs, science, as the Egyptians left their kings and symbolic gods in the sepulchres of Thebes and Memphis. The future brings its aspirations, its seeds wrapped in a developing language and in splendid poetry; a mysterious child who drinks from two breasts the milk of sacred tradition and profane fiction, Moses and St Paul, Homer and Virgil..."

It should be noted that Dante was the inventor of an idiom that his genius filled with grace and energy. "A double genius, he created a poem without equal and a magnificent language whose secret he kept. Whatever its influence on the literary language of Italy, it nevertheless kept its own special character which made it exclusively his. It is particularly remarkable for its clarity and preciseness, and for a certain unique brevity and vividness. In some ways it reflects Dante's genius: it is vigorous, concise and wholly unpretentious. Everything is abbreviated, transmitting ideas, feelings and images from his soul and mind to other souls and minds by a sort of direct of communication, almost without the need for words".

All the miniatures in the magnificent manuscript that is published here for the first time were executed in the 15th century. The masterpiece is kept in the Biblioteca Nazionale Marciana in Venice.

Hell

No human being has ever returned from the terrifying forest where Dante is lost. After an entire night of anguish, the Poet arrives at the foot of a mountain bathed in sunlight. He believes himself to be out of danger when three wild beasts, a leopard, a lion and a she-wolf suddenly step into his path. It is the famished, rawboned wolf that is most determined to make him retreat to the woods. It is at this moment that a man, or rather a shade, appears. Although he has no idea who it is, Dante calls for his help.

"My parents were from Mantova, and I who lived during the reign of Augustus sang the songs of Aeneas, son of Anchises"... the stranger replies, and Dante immediately recognizes Virgil, whom he always considered to be his inspiration. So, ashamed of having fled the wild beasts, he implores the author of the Aeneid to do all he can to let him reach the mountain. Virgil advises him to take another path which leads to Paradise, via Hell and Purgatory. He offers to guide him to the kingdom of the Chosen for as long as Providence deems it wise.

Virgil and Dante at the gates of Hell. The entire edifice, except the gate, has been treated with sepia. The architectural motifs are borrowed from Altichiero. (Canto II and III.)

Dante is all the more thankful for this invitation as his mentor tells him that Beatrice has interceded on his behalf and will welcome him in Heaven. He accepts to undertake the journey with joy. At the gates of Hell is a warning that rings out like a threat: Abandon hope, all ye who enter here. Dante is overwrought and will only enter on Virgil's

...a dicitu(n) die ecamea(n)e
...cucta tu signore tu maestro
...lidissi e poi che mosso fue
...tra p(er) locammo alto esiluestro

Em(e) sina nella cicradolente
...ime sina nellecerno dolore

Top left, the two Poets walk across an endless plain. On the right is Pluto at a doorstep carved from the rock. In the lower miniature, Prodigals and the Greedy carry heavy rocks on their shoulders. (Canto VI and VII.)

Right: Phlegyas ferries Dante and Virgil across Acheron in his boat. Two towers can be seen (though Dante speaks only of one). Built on both banks of the river of Hell, they are topped by a small flame. Filippo Argenti is rocking the boat wildly because he is arguing with Dante. The artist's skill can be seen in the way he draws (from behind) the angry sinner's head. (Canto VIII.)

insistence. The latter takes him by the hand and calms him, with a smile.

Both make their way into the frightening darkness torn by lamentations, sighs and cries of despair. This grim introduction puts Dante into a state of distress. His guide explains that these are the souls of the Apathetic, those who lived "without praise or infamy" and who were rejected by both Heaven and Hell. Having never done the good that they could have done, they are condemned to be goaded by a storm of fierce insects, whose sting is horrifying. A little further, a crowd of the damned is huddled on the bank of Acheron, waiting for old Charon, the ferryman, to take them across the river in his boat. As soon as he sees the two pilgrims, the boatman shouts to them to hurry on board. On the other bank they will find the everlasting darkness, the heat and the cold. But, on noticing that Dante is alive, the old man becomes angry. To calm him, Virgil has to explain that his companion's fate is desired by Heaven, where all desires come true.

Dante, Virgil and the city of Dis. The architectural details were inspired by the oratory of St George in Padua, which was designed by Altichiero da Zevio, an Italian painter of the 14th century, who also worked in Verona. The details copied can be noted in the scene where the saint, surrounded by this peers, presents Raimondino Lupi to the Virgin. The artist has perfectly reproduced the trefoil opening of the three-pointed fronton, which is a characteristic of the building, as well as the motifs decorating the chapel dedicated to Saint James in the basilica at Padua. The Furies are at the top of the small tower. The signature on the two gratings cannot be read. (Cantos VIII and IX.)

However, souls continue to board the boat, swearing and crying, while others congregate on the bank. There is a great roar, followed by an earthquake, which shakes the gates of Hell. Frightened out of his wits, Dante faints.

When he awakes once more, the Poet notices that he is on the other side of Acheron. His Master invites him to continue until the First Circle—Limbo—where are gathered those who never received the true faith, as they were born before the time of Christ. Dante recognizes Homer, Horace and Ovid, and stops for a moment to talk with these great men, who honored poetry so. But night is falling fast as they reach the Second Circle, which is guarded by Minos, who also has the task of judging the damned. To indicate to each one the circle to which he is assigned, he wraps his tail round himself the number of grades that the person has to go down. Shouts and moans are mixed with the roar of the eternal hurricane. In the Second Circle are the Lustful, hurled round by a storm and never given a moment of peace. It is thus that the souls of Paolo and Francesca, tightly held against each other as they were when death surprised them, come towards the two travelers. Moved to tears, Dante learns that the Book of Galahad, which tells the tale of the love of Lancelot and Guinevere, awoke passion and desire in them, leading them to exchange a kiss, which made them commit mortal sin and brought about their death.

Dante and his protector soon come to the Third Circle, guarded by Cerebus, a three-headed monster, who flails and rends the Gluttonous, who are dipped in stinking mud. Again, Virgil has to use his influence to let Pluto allow them through without hindrance. Only the assurance that the divine will has decided on this descent into Hell persuades him to stand aside and let them pass. In the next circle are the Hoarders and the Spendthrifts, who are condemned to roll boulders by pushing them with their breasts. In the first group Dante notices a number of popes and cardinals, but cannot recognize any of them. Virgil claims that the reason is that during their lives their greed had already squashed in them all knowledge that had nothing to do with their obsession.

The Wrathful and Vengeful are plunged into the marshes of Styx, another of Hell's rivers. Some tear their bodies to pieces by biting themselves, while others, completely covered in slime, admit their crime, and with each of their words comes the obscene gurgling of the putrid water in which they are imprisoned. Fleeing this appalling spectacle, Dante sees before him a high tower at the top of which shine two flames, and he notices a skiff, piloted by Phlegyas. Thanks to him, the two pilgrims to Hell get to the other bank and the city of Dis, in which are the damned who have committed the most mortal sins. During the trip, a furious voice comes from the pool. It is that of a captive, astonished that a living man has been allowed to visit the

Virgil, Dante, Phlegyas and Styx. The Angel crosses Styx. The arches resemble those by the artist who painted the "Life of Saint Louis of Toulouse" in the Visconti oratory in Albizzata. The brushwork and the lightness of touch in the relief are remarkable. In this landscape of arches—each of which is a tomb—stands the solitary and powerful shape of Farinata (see plate 7v). To accentuate the majesty of this central figure, the drawing of Cavalcante de Cavalcanti can hardly be seen. (Canto IX, v. 104-133.)

kingdom of the dead. The man is none other than Filippo Argenti, Dante's personal enemy. Drunk with pride when he was on earth, he is now like a pig wallowing in the mire.

At the gates of the city of Dis more than a thousand threatening and fierce devils mount the guard. They intend not to let the visitors in and shout to them that they will not allow them through. This time the Master's words are without effect. Virgil may go through if he wishes, but not Dante. And to dissuade them from going further, three Furies at the top of the tower, with hair made of snakes and faces covered with blood, hurl insults at them.

An awful roaring comes from the waters of Styx, announcing the arrival of a divine messenger. The souls of the damned fell him in horror. The demons give in, and the Angel, with one blow of his staff, opens the gates of Dis.

Left: Dante, Virgil and Farinata. Dante's text notes that Farinata's strong body stands "from the waist to the top" in a lonely landscape. The arches or tombs resemble those in the painting of the "Life of Saint Louis" in the Visconti oratory in Albizzata.

Above: The Heretics. The two Poets are already on the inner edge of the Sixth Circle. The Soul in torment that they meet is in a tomb, which, strange to relate, is not in flames. Dressed in a white pontifical alb, with a red robe and slippers of the same color, this is Anastasius II to whom Dante, according to an erroneous tradition, attributes the sin of heresy. (Canto XI.)

Dante and his guide enter the Sixth Circle where heretics expiate their sins lying in burning tombs. Recognizing him by his Florentine accent, one of the damned rises and shows himself to the Poet: it is Farinata degli Uberti. He recalls the Battle of Montaperti (1260), won by the Ghibellines and which nearly led to the destruction of Florence, then launches into a heated political debate with Dante.

More than a thousand sufferers are gathered in this place, but the guest of Hell can only speak to the father of his friend Guido Cavalcanti and to Frederick II, emperor of Naples and Sicily.

An unbearable stench hangs over the edge of the cliff which separates the Sixth from the Seventh Circle. To escape from it, Dante hides behind a tomb. It belongs to Anastasius II, the pope who accepted the heresy of Photinus, who claimed that Christ was only a man. Questioned by his disciple, Virgil explains how the damned are divided up in the next circles. The most terrible punishment is reserved for traitors, who are in the smallest and deepest circle.

Nessus, Chiron, Pholus. The Violent are plunged in the Phlegethon, a river of boiling blood. The are guarded by Centaurs which shoot arrows at them each time they come out further than their punishment allows. "O blind greed, O crazy anger That spur us on in this life so brief, Is it to have us burn for life eternal? ... And I, back bent, saw a great trench Which embraced the whole universe." The trench can be seen below. (Canto XII, v. 46-48.)

Right: The Violent against themselves (Suicides) and against their own goods (Profligates). Pier della Vigna. The branches, without leaves, are the nests of the Harpies, the monsters with a woman's head and a bird's body. (Canto XIII, v. 25-73.)

redo che e credette ch'io credesse
che tante uoce uscisser tra que brochi
dagente ch'epnoi si nascondesse

Above: The Violent against Nature (Sodomites) Brunetto Latini (Dante's master, author of "Les Livres dou Trésor"), Prisciano, Francesco d'Accursio. (Canto XV.)

Right: Geryon, the Monster of Fraud, has the face of an honest man but the body of a dragon-snake with a long and poisonous tail. Virgil speaks to him and asks him to take them down to the Eighth Circle. There the Poets meet the Usurers, who are Violent against Nature, daughter of God, and Art, nephew of God.

The Usurers are seated and use their hands to protect themselves from the fire of rain. Three of them can be recognized by the purse that hangs round their neck and which bears the emblem of their family: an azure lion on a field of gold for the Gianfigliazzi (perhaps in this case Catello di Rosso); a white goose on a field of gules for the Ebriachi (it is believed to be Ciappo); an azure sow on a white field for the third, probably Reginaldo degli Scrovegni, a famous usurer of the time. (Canto XVII, v. 10-18.)

Having become accustomed to the putrid smells which rise from the depths, the two friends continue their journey. The descent is by a steep path, and made more dangerous by the presence of the Minotaur. But Virgil only has to remind him of the miserable end that Theseus, helped by Ariadne, brought upon him, for the monster to become mad. The two poets, taking advantage of this, enter the Seventh Circle. Before them stretches the third river of Hell, the Phlegethon, a river of boiling blood in which those violent against their neighbor are immersed. Their torture is aggravated by a herd of centaurs, which shoot arrows from the bank at those who try to flee. Among the tyrants and murderers, Dante recognizes the cruel Ezzelino da Romano and also Guy de Montfort, who murdered Prince Henry of England in Viterbo Cathedral. The centaur Chiron willingly accepts to help Dante cross the river and orders Nessus to take him on his back and lead him to the strange and sinister wood which is on the other side.

Harpies, horrible birds with womens' faces, perched on the branches of the trees, shriek at the poets as they go past. Hearing sobs, the Florentine thinks that the souls of the damned are behind the trees, but this is not so. "Just cut a little branch", says his Master. He has hardly obeyed when a cry of pain comes from the tree. "Why are you dismembering me? asks the soul who is prisoner there. It is Pier della Vigna, who committed suicide in the gaol of Frederick II, whose secretary and confidant he was, and who had imprisoned him on false suspicions. But this did not enable him to escape the punishment for those who commit suicide. The forest is also full of profligates who run around followed by starving dogs.

Each manifestation of the sin of violence is marked by its own punishment. Thus, the violent against God, Nature and Art lay in a desert of sand on which fire rains. Following the bank of the Phlegethon, Dante meets a group of souls, one of whom, intrigued, stops. It is Brunetto Latini who tells his former pupil of the misfortunes caused by his fellow citizens, envious and proud people. He also tells Dante to continue with his "Treasure" (i.e., his literary work).

The two visitors continue their walk, to the roar of the river which falls into the abyss of the Eighth Circle. The sight of this makes the Poet dizzy, but the monster which rises from the depths strikes terror into his heart. This is Geryon, a creature with a man's head on a snake's body covered in scales and ending in a forked tail bristling with stings. The awful beast stops on the edge of the gulf. While Dante goes to speak with the shades of Usurers, Virgil tries to convince the fabled beast to carry them to the bottom of his den. Geryon accepts, but warns Dante that he must cling tightly to his back. This Dante does and as soon as they are airborne, he is overcome by fear and his senses reel.

The gloomy rock of Maleboge now surrounds the two Poets. At its centre is the black mouth of a well which leads to the ten trenches that form the Eighth Circle. They first meet the Seducers, scourged by demons, then the Panderers, who are plunged into dung. Among these unfortunates are Alessio Interminelli

DISSIO CCLX
Er elliame s
iagiu pque
ualui sa pa

The Flatterers. They are plunged in excrement which seems to have been "taken from men's latrines". Dante talks with Alession Interminelli from Lucca. Virgil then urges him to look at Thais, the Athenian harlot, taken by Terence in the play Eunuchus. In the play, Thrason asks his servant and go-between, Gnaton, if Thais, to whom he has sent the present of a young slave musician, has thanked him. "Yes, very much" is the reply. (Canto XVIII, v. 114.)

The Third Trench is in the lower part of the illustration, showing the Simoniacs. "Then we came to the following tomb. And we clmbed to the summit of the rock Which hung over the middle of the trench." The Simoniacs are planted head down in holes dug in the rock. Their feet stick out and writhe violently when the flames burn them. At the bottom, four Simoniacs are stuck in two ancient baptismal fonts. Dante questions one of them, and finds out that it none other than Pope Nicholas III Orsini, who mistakes him for a soul in torment and even thinks he is Pope Boniface VIII. On the right we see Dante lifted onto Virgil's shoulders carried down a steep slope to the Fourth Trench, that of Sorcerers. (Canto XIX, v. 7-9.)

Phais, the prostitute. In the third bowge, the Simoniacs expiate their sins. They are damned for having traded sacred objects and are set head down in holes with only their feet outside tickled by a short tongue of flame. This is the fate of several popes, including Nicholas III, whom Dante rebukes. It is their greed for gold, he claims, thet is the cause of all the ills that humanity has to bear. Equally as guilty as the Simoniacs are the Sorcerers who have spent their lives trying to read the future. Now, their head is turned backwards, condemned to look behind them for eternity. The Poet is so moved by this scene that Virgil upbraids him for his compassion. It is then that they discover, below them, a lake of boiling black pitch, where are thrown the prisoners of the fifth trench. These are Extortioners,

Above: The Barrators. The two Poets arrive at the bridge of the Fifth Trench, which is a pool of boiling pitch. The barrators are tortured by particularly nasty devils. One of them carried a man from Lucca on his shoulders and throws him into the pitch where the other demons playfully push him in. Virgil warns Dante and advises him to hide in a hollow, while protecting him with his body and parleying with Beelzebub, delegated by the other devils to speak with him. (Canto XXI.)

Below: The Hypocrites. Virgil, carrying Dante, descends the steep slope that leads to the Sixth Trench. "And now we saw a people decked with paint, Who trod their circling way with tear and groan." Dante questions the souls in torment. "Our orange-gilded dress Is leaden, and so heavy that its weight Wrings out these creakings from the balances. Two jovial friars were we; our city-state Bologna." The soul in torment on the cross on the ground is Caiaphas. (Canto XXIII.)

The Counsellors of Fraud. Ulysses and Diomede. A bright red flame, on which brown spots can nevertheless be seen, surrounds the bodies of Ulysses and Diomede and draws attention to them. Dante is burning to speak to the two heroes of ancient times, but it is Virgil who asks the questions, standing in front of Ulysses. The shade of the hero of the Odyssey tells of the voyage that led him past the Pillars of Hercules and the end of this mad undertaking through which he hoped to find virtue and knowedge. (Canto XXIV.)

guarded by devils, armed with grapples which they use to pitilessly strike any shade who tries to reach the bank. The ten demons who are on guard escort the two pilgrims to the embankment which overlooks the abyss, quarrelling all the time. Dante and Virgil thus pass without trouble into the next trench, where a group of shades advances slowly towards them. These are Hypocrites. For having dissimulated their intentions throughout their whole life, they are condemned to stagger under the weight of capes which are wrapped round them, the outside of which shines like gold, while the inside is vulgar lead. Not far away, the high priest Caiaphas, who advised the Pharisees to put Christ to death, lies cricufied across the path, continually trodden on by the feet of the passing damned.

Dante is exhausted by his trials as much as by tiredness and he cannot climb the steep slope that leads to the entrance of the Seventh Trench. Virgil urges him on, saying that it is not by sleeping that he will gain his honors! He has to suffer and perservere. The Florentine agrees and they both set off together towards the jail where the Thieves are kept. Snakes of all kinds coil around them, squeezing their bodies in a knot. If any tries to escape, he is stung by one of the reptiles and turns into a heap of dust. One of these is Vanni Fucci of Pistoia, who has stolen sacred objects from the church of St James.

The sufferings of the False Counsellors, who are thrown into the Eighth Trench, are hardly less cruel. They burn like faggots in an eternal fire. Sent to Hell for having thought up and carried out the most subtle tricks during the siege of Troy, Diomedes and Ulysses are captives of a forked flame, the tips of which run around them both. The hero of the Odyssey tells Dante of the adventures of his last journey. Inspired by the unique and noble wish to improve his knowledge, he had just gone past the Pillars of Hercules (the Straits of Gibraltar) when a storm overturned his boat and sent him to the bottom of the sea.

The Ninth Trench is occupied by the Sowers of Discord and Schismatics. The horror of the place is almost beyond description. A devil smites the victims asunder with his sword, and the damned are forced to return each time for more punishment. Mahomet and his nephew Ali are among the tortured. The Prophet shows his wounds to Dante.

A gloomy and thick night reigns over the Tenth and last Trench, from which emanate screams so atrocious that the Poet is forced to cover his ears with his hands. The screams belong to the Falsifiers, tricksters and liars of all kinds who are plagued by leprosy, rabies and other hideous diseases. One of them, Griffolino d'Arezzo, executed for having made Alberto da Siena believe that he could teach him to steal like a bird, was sent to Hell as an alchemist. Sinon, who convinced the Trojans to let the famous wooden horse into the city, is stricken with a violent fever. Beside him is the wife of Potiphar, who, according to the Bible, unjustly accused Joseph of having dishonored her.

Left: The Sowers of Scandal and Schism. The miniature shows Mahomet from the front: his body is cut open from nose to belly, his guts hanging out and spilling around him. (Canto XXVIII, v. 31-33.)

Above: The Sowers of Scandal and Schism. Falsifiers of metal and coins. Among the first souls in torment, who are laid on the ground their bodies covered in sores, Dante sees one of his relations stand up. It is Geri del Bello, who, with a threatening air, points at him.

The miniature on the following page shows two souls in torment sitting apart on a rock, scratching themselves furiously. One is Griffolino d'Areezo, an alchemist; the other, Capocchio, a forger. The first has been burnt alive for having promised to teach the son of the bishop of Sienna to steal like a bird, but it is because he was an alchemist that he is in this part of Hell. Capocchio also did penance for his crimes at the stake. Note the expressive vigor of the naked bodies of the damned and Virgil's harsh attitude. (Canto XXIX, v. 13-39 and 73-120.)

The travelers have passed from the Eight to the Ninth Circle without the darkness lifting. Dante sees a wall, above which he thinks he can see high towers. But the Master explains to him that in fact these are Giants who are trying to climb to Heaven. Chained to the bottom of an enormous well, they can harm no one except Antaeus. It is this man who takes his guests by the hand and leads them to the last Circle, that of Cocytus.

The Giants. This is a scene full of movement which shows the Giants rebelling against Jupiter. To punish them, the god has chained them and thrown them in a well, where they are changed into towers. They only look big in comparison to Dante and Virgil, who Antaeus has agreed to take to the Eighth Circle.

Among the furrowed and powerful faces of the Giants drawn in profile, one is face on; for this one, the artist seems to have taken inspiration from the face of the Zeus of Otricoli. (Canto XXXI, v. 43-45.)

Traitors to their country. In a frozen cove of the Lake Cocytus are plunged traitors, some of them lying on their stomachs, others on their backs. Dante asks one of them his name and, as the man refuses to answer, grabs him by the hair to make him speak. The man is stubborn and resists, but another traitor calls him by his name: Bocca degli Abati. (Canto XXXII, v. 97-102.)

Here is a frozen lake into which traitors are plunged. The place is so dreary that to describe it Dante has to ask for the help of the Muses before carefully treading on the ice to avoid stepping on the heads of the damned. Among them he recognizes his compatriot Sassolo Mascheroni, murderer of his own nephew whose inheritance he coveted, and Camicion de Pazzi, murderer of his cousin Ubertino. He inadvertently strikes the head of one of the sufferers, who pleads with him not to add to the woes that he is enduring for having betrayed his own side at the battle of Montaperti. His interest aroused, he stops and asks the man's name. As the man refuses, Dante grabs him by the hair to force him to speak, but another sinner tells him that the man is Bocca degli Abbati, whose treachery led to the defeat of the Guelphs by the Ghibellines.

Then follows a sight of abominable cruelty: a shade is seen eating the head of one of his companions. When the Florentine asks why there is such cruelty, he is answered by Count Ugolino, who tells the tale of his tragic end. Imprisoned in the Gualandi tower in Pisa by Bishop Ruggieri, himself, his sons, and his nephews were starved to death by the ignoble prelate. Moved to tears, Dante curses the city, which he calls the "shame of all people".

To reach the last of Hell's provinces, the two pilgrims have to fray a path through the other damned, who are frozen in the ice to their very tears.

Traitors to their country. The artist has drawn Count Ugolino della Gherardesca, who betrayed Pisa before himself being duped by Archbishop Roger, who left him to die in a tower. Although guilty himself, Ugolino is used as an executor of divine justice: he is seen biting Roger's head with beastly cruelty. The archbishop's mitre, hemmed with red, can be seen lying on the ground, a reminder of ecclesiastic dignity. The two Poets, holding each other tight, look on horrified. (Canto XXXIII, v. 1-78.)

Traitors to their guests. We are in the Ptolomaea, a frozen region of Cocytus, where traitors against their guests are punished. One of the souls, who can be recognized by his head which is slightly lifted, asks Dante to remove the veil of ice which covers his eyes. The Poet promises to do so, as long as the man speaks. And this is what Alberigo dei Manfredi does; to take revenge on his brother and his nephew, his political enemies, he invited them to a banquet to make peace, but at the end of which he murdered them. Dante did not keep his word: "It was a courtesy to be nasty to him." (Canto XXXIII, v. 150.)

Lucifer. The drawing which shows Lucifer is lightly shaded but sustained by sanguine features. We are at the center of the Earth in the nether region of Cocytus, Judecca, reserved for traitors to their lords. Lucifer is a huge giant with the wings of a bat. His head has three faces and as many mouths. The one in the middle devours Judas, who betrayed Christ; the two others, Brutus and Cassius, who betrayed the trust of Caesar. The bodies of the other souls in torment are set in the ice in various positions. On the left, Dante and Virgil observe the scene. Below, they can be seen holding on to the hair of the king of Hell rising to the other hemisphere. (Canto XXXIV.)

They have now arrived at the heart of kingdom of Lucifer, the angel who was thrown from Heaven by God to the center of the Earth. The King of the Demons is huge and terrifying. Each of his three mouths crunches the body of a damned person and at the same time his sharp claws tear them apart. This is the fate of three of the greatest traitors of all time: Judas, Brutus and Cassius.

The extraordinary voyage among the "lost people" has come to its end. Carefully going down the length of Lucifer's body, Dante and Virgil finally come to a narrow corridor by which they climb until they can see the stars again.

48

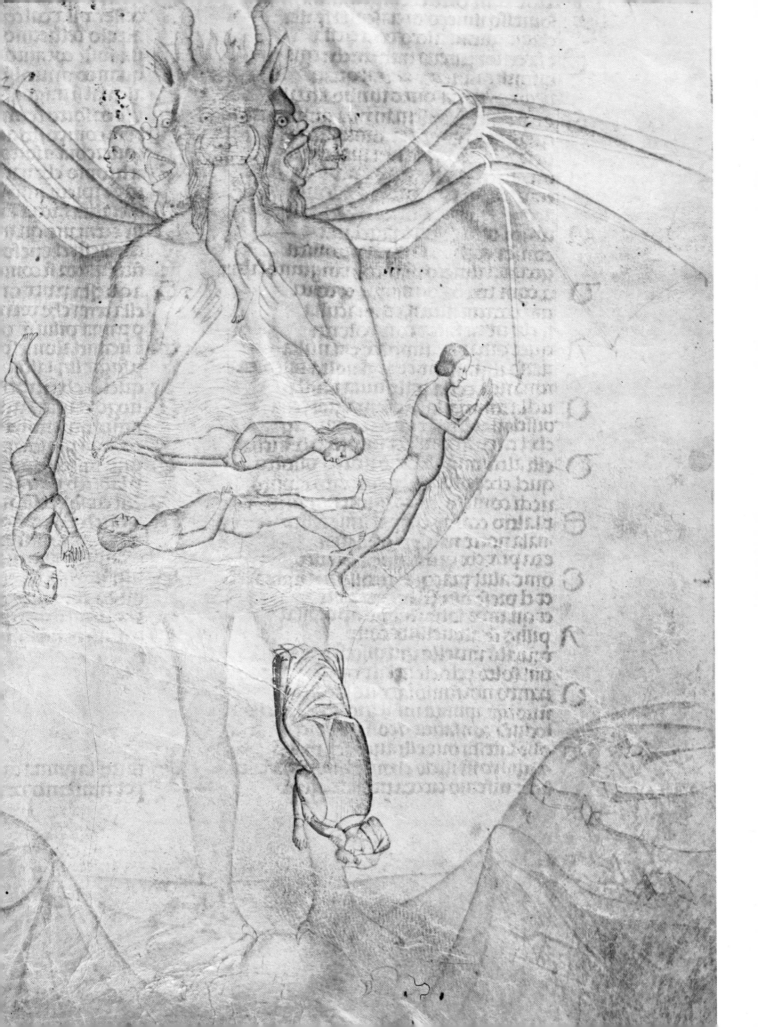

Purgatory

Dante discovers a calm and serene scene when he sets foot on Purgatory's beach. The reign of darkness is in the past. This fact gives him the impression of being reborn and he feels ready to continue his journey to the end in Virgil's company.

A noble old man comes towards the two poets. This is Cato, keeper of this place where souls free themselves of their sins to make themselves worthy of going to Heaven. Cato willingly gives them permission to visit this place of penance, but tells Virgil to first wash his disciple to cleanse him of the filth of Hell. Once this rite is finished, they look around them, not knowing which way to take. An Angel appears in a flash of blinding whiteness; it is he who ferries repentant souls into Ante-purgatory on his boat. His passengers are surprised by Dante's presence; they can guess he is human from his breathing. One of them comes with open arms to the Poet, who recognizes his friend Casella, a talented Florentine musician. But when he tries to embrace him, Dante finds only thin air. Casella sings one of Dante's songs "Love which speaks in the depths of my soul" in a magnificent voice. The shades fall into a state of ecstasy, until Cato comes and upbraids them for delaying the start of their penance. Showing them the mountain of Purgatory, he tells them that they must stay there until they are purified. The procession begins and the travelers join it. The difficulties begin as soon as they arrive at the foot of the hill. The rocky slope is so steep that it is impossible to climb. While they are wondering how to go about it, a group of souls appears. Virgil asks them for the easiest way.

Dante's purification. In a spring landscape, with a river bank and, in the background, some small golden flowers with long stems, Virgil girds the Poet, who has just passed through the infernal regions, with the "pure rush". He carries out this sacramental gesture on Cato's orders, as Dante has to be purified of the murk and contamination of Hell. The operation takes place in an idyllic landscape lit by the light of early morning. This Easter Sunday decor has been stressed by the miniaturist with the floral embellishment which surrounds the entire upper part of the illustration. (Canto I, v. 94-100.)

Below: Ante-purgatory. In the first scene, the ferrying angel has already taken Dante and Virgil across, and is preparing to take other waiting souls. (Canto II, v. 13-36.)

Following pages: In the first scene, Dante and Virgil talk with the souls of the dead. Among them, Dante recognizes his friend Casella, the singer (v. 91-105). In the second, Cato upbraids the souls for their lack of haste. (Canto II, v. 118-133.)

The shades are surprised that Dante's body stops the sun's rays. One of the shades steps forward and asks Dante to look at him. He has a wound on his forehead and another above his heart. He is blond-haired and has a noble bearing. It is Manfred, the heroic son of Frederick II, who died at the battle of Benevento. He tells of his end, and how, at the moment of death, he commended his soul to God, who pardoned his sins. Listening to the story, the Florentine loses all idea of time. His guide urges him to go on and tells him that he will be able to rest before reaching the summit of the mountain.

Around them, in sitting positions, or lying down, are the souls of the Negligent and the Lazy who mutter among themselves as the Poet goes by. Braver than the other souls, Buonconte da Montefeltro asks Dante to remember him in his prayers so that he will be absolved sooner of his sins. He was killed at the battle of Campaldino, but neither his wife Constance nor his relations have prayed for the salvation of his soul. Pia dei Tolomei also addresses the same request to Dante.

Dante then directs his Master's attention to a stranger, who is standing disdainfully aside from the others. But when Virgil tells him that he is from Mantova, the man approaches and kisses him. He is from the same city and is called Sordello, a poet who wrote in local dialect. The meeting with Dante provides him with the opportunity to shower insults on the hateful factions which divide Italy, when it would be so easy if everyone were to consider himself as belonging to the same country and to like each other without necessarily knowing each other, thus following Sordello's example. The latter joins them, and together they cross a marvelous valley of flowers. Two angels guard it carrying swords to keep away the Devil, who will soon

Left: At the foot of the mountain, Dante and Virgil discover a large group of souls who are formed in two lines. These are souls dead in default of the Church. A little further, towards the right on a knoll, is Manfredi, the natural son of Frederick II, who reigned over Sicily from 1250 to 1266 and was defeated by Charles of Anjou, who came to Italy at the invitation of Pope Clement IV. (Canto III.)

Below: The souls crowd around Dante. They plead with him to recall their memory to their relations still alive so that prayers can be said to help them. (Canto IV, v. 10-12.)

return to tempt the penitent. In fact, shortly afterwards, the horrible animal appears in the grass. Luckily, the Seraphim see it and chase it out. Suddenly exhausted, Dante closes his eyes and lies on the grass, where he falls asleep. He dreams that an eagle swoops down on him, picks him up and carries him towards a ball of fire. The heat that he feels is so great that he wakes up and looks around him in fear. Virgil calms him. While

In the Valley of Neglectful Princes (who repented before dying), the souls recite evening prayers; they form a tight group placed in the center of the first scene. Above them float two guardian angels. On the right, Dante talks to Nino Visconti, who was his friend and who asks to be remembered to his daughter. In the second scene, Dante talks to Corrado Malaspina, whose descendants are to welcome Dante with great friendship during his exile. Signed with a flourish, the miniature is valuable for the animation and energetic beauty of the faces represented. (Canto IV, v. 1-18; 19-42; 43-84; 109-139.)

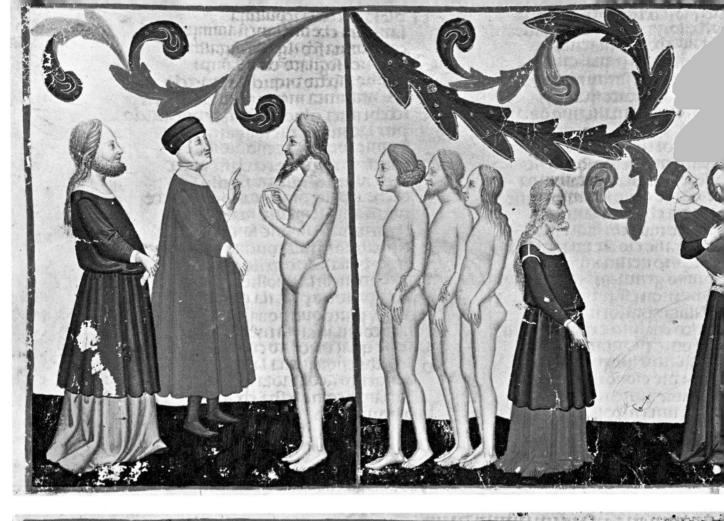

he was sleeping, Lucy has come down from Heaven, taken him in her arms and laid him outside the gates of Purgatory, where they now find themselves.

An Angel stands before him. A bright light shines from his face. He holds a flashing sword. Having learnt of Lucy's act, he draws the letter "P" seven times on Dante's forehead to symbolize the Seven Capital Sins which the Poet must wash away while climbing the mountain. Then, with keys of gold and silver, he opens the gates of Purgatory.

The Master and his pupil slowly make their way along a winding path cut out of the rock before coming to the center of a circle. All around them are walls of white marble, with scenes from the Bible, mythology and history showing examples of humility and pride sculpted on them. They are now on the First Cornice, where those punished for their pride are kept. While Dante admires the sculptures, a group of shades arrives. All are bent under the weight of heavy rocks, and, reciting the Our Father, beat their breasts. At each step they seem to be on the point of falling and not being able to get up again.

With a great effort, one of them manages to raise his eyes towards Dante, whom he recognizes. It is Odderisi da Gubbio, a famous miniature painter, who was guilty of pride, and flattered himself that he was one of the greatest artists of his time. Now he humbly acknowledges the greatness of Franco Bolognese, reminding men of the vanity of the things of this world.

The Arrogant. The high reliefs of decorated white marble, which illustrate three scenes from the Old Testament (David dancing in honor of God before the Ark and the Tables of the Law); from the Gospel (a delicately painted Annunciation); and from Roman history, where the emperor Trajan, on the point of leaving for war, does justice for a widow whose son has been murdered. These are found in the First Cornice of the Arrogant.

Virgil and Dante admire this triptych. The work is very much in the style of Altichiero. The expression, elegance and color are quite admirable. (Canto X, v. 28-93.)

Right: The Arrogant punished. Because they kept their bodies and souls too "erect" during their life on Earth, the Arrogant are made to carry a great rock on their back, wich bends them in two and keeps their faces to the ground. Among them, Dante recognizes (during the next Canto) Oderisida Gubbio, an excellent miniaturist from Umbria, known for his burning desire to always be first. Now he is condemned to humbly recognize that Franco Bolognese's art was better than his. This is an act of contrition but also perhaps a good critical judgment, although no work by either of these artists has been positively identified. (Canto X, v. 115-117.)

An Angel with its wings spread appears to the travelers to show them the staircase which will take them to the Second Cornice, where the Envious do penance. They wear hair shirts and their eyelids are sewn with wire. Dante recognizes some of them: Sappia from Sienna, who, during her life, rejoiced in the misfortunes of others; Guida del Duca and Rinieri da Caboli, who complain bitterly of the moral decadence of their native province, Romagna, where so many illustrious souls once lived.

The climb to the Second Cornice, that of the Envious. The two Poets, after having passed in front of other groups of the Arrogant and after observing other examples of punished vanity, see the Angel of Humility coming from Heaven. He is dressed in red with big blue wings. He shows them the road which leads to the Second Cornice. Dante begins to climb using a ladder which leans against a small hill. Virgil follows him. The miniature across the bottom of the page is noteworthy for its beautiful colors and elegant lines. (Canto XII, v. 115-136.)

To the right the two Poets are called by two spirits, Guido del Duca and Rinieri da Calboli, who are surprised that a living being has managed to reach the kingdom of the dead. In the two scenes, the characters are brilliantly drawn with a wide range of expressions on the faces and in the attitude of the bodies. (Canto XIV, v. 1-24.)

The climb to the Third Cornice. The angel of mercy, come down from Heaven unexpectedly, and whose arrival brightens the light of the sun at dusk, shows the Poets the easiest staircase to climb to reach the Third Cornice. This privilege is accorded to Dante because the weight of his sins has already diminished. The three figures appear solitary and clear on the part of the parchment which has kept its natural color: ivory white. (Canto XV, v. 1-39.)

Virgil and his companion continue their way among the penitents whose lamentations and moans plunge Dante into a state of profound worry. But, soon after, he is blinded by a light so bright that is he forced to cover his eyes with his hands. It is another Angel come to show them the staircase which leads to the Third Cornice. Here are kept the Irritable, wrapped in a thick cloud of smoke. As if in contrast, Dante has ecstatic visions which are all examples of good. First he sees the Virgin Mary, who having found her son among the doctors in the temple, speaks to him gently. Then St Stephen appears. He was the first martyr and he prays for his executioners even as the crowd stones him to death. When the Poet comes to, it is night. When a voice asks him who he is, he replies and the shade also gives his name. He is Marco Lombardo, who lived in the court of Lombardy. Dante approves when the man attributes the corruption of the world to the scandalous behavior of popes and to the confusion between temporal and spiritual power.

As the pilgrims continue their way, the cloud slowly disappears. New visions come to Dante. The souls of those dead for their sins appear to him: Aman, whom Assuerus put to death on the cross for having massacred the Hebrews; Procnea, who, through revenge, killed her son and made her husband eat his flesh; Amata, wife of King Latinus, who killed herself to avoid seeing her daughter Lavinia marry Aenaeus.

Following pages: The Angry. Examples of good. The miniature is made up of four small scenes, drawn with much elegance and easy to understand. Dante is in ecstasy before four visions which appear to him. At top left, the child Jesus with the doctors of the Law; right, Joseph and Mary find their son. Below, left, Pisistrates, against his wife's will forgiving a young man who has kissed his daughter; finally, right, the stoning of Saint Stephen. (Canto XV, v. 82-93.)

espoder la conuiso teiupato

The Angry. Examples of anger. As an example of anger, the artist has chosen the episode of Queen Amata, who kills herself because she did not want to see her daughter, whose fiancé was believed dead, forced to marry Aenaeus, their enemy. This is one of Dante's visions, and so he is shown with eyes closed and a hand to his face. This is a signed miniature. (Canto XVII, v. 35-39.)

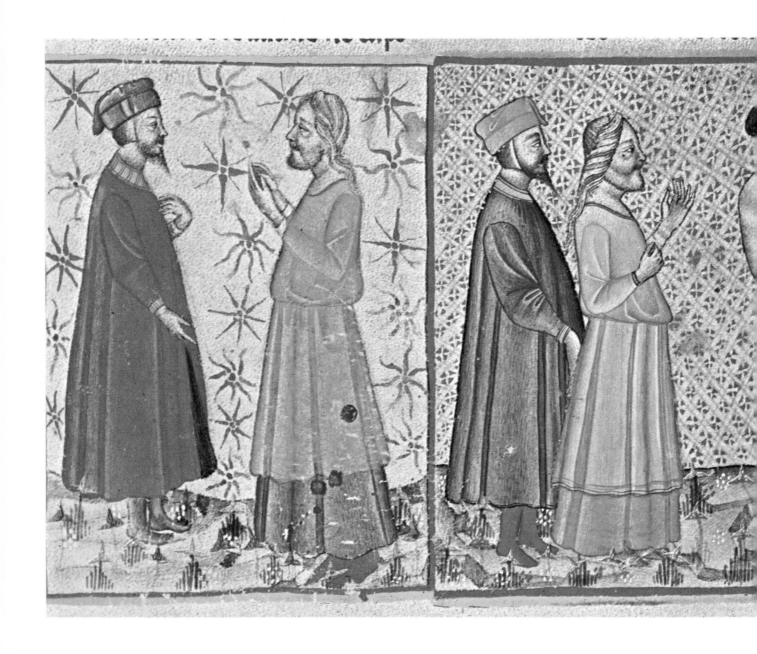

The Lazy. The Abbot of San Zeno. Virgil asks for the way which leads to the Fifth Cornice with the souls of the Lazy, whose punishment is to run without stopping. The Abbot of the monastery of San Zeno, who is last in the group of penitents, kindly informs him, before complaining about those who have inherited his position after his death. (Canto XVIII, v. 106-129.)

Right: Between the Fourth and Fifth Cornice. The angel of ardent charity towards God comes down from the sky and encourages Dante and Virgil to continue their climb. There is no longer a staircase, which probably means that Dante is climbing with greater ease. As Virgil asks his companion why he looks so thoughtful, Dante replies: "Because of a dream". And Virgil interprets this new vision. (Canto XIX, v. 34-51.)

This time Dante is awakened by the light of an Angel, who invites him to come to the Fourth Cornice. On the way, Virgil reveals to his disciple the theory and nature of love, the meaning of free will and the moral structures of Purgatory. He tells him that Beatrice is waiting in Paradise to continue his teaching in these subjects.

Outdoing each other in enthusiasm, a group of penitents appears shouting out a thousand examples of mildness. These are the Lazy, who lost their lives through sinning by indolence. This was the fate of the Hebrews who fell in the desert because they refused to follow Moses to the land of Canaan. Again Dante is overcome by tiredness, falls asleep and dreams. A horrible woman changes before his eyes into a seductive siren, but a young girl arrives and unmasks her; later Virgil explains the meaning of this strange dream. But

The Greedy and Prodigal are laid on their stomach, hands and feet bound. They weep and moan while reciting the words of the Palmist : "Adhaesit pavimento anima mea" ("My soul is tied to the ground," Ps. CXVIII, 25). One of the spirits, Adrian V (Ottobruno Fieschi, who was pope for 38 days, from 11 July to 18 August 1276) explains to Dante the reason why they have to do such penance: for having enjoyed without shame the possession of riches in the world, they are oblig-ed to stare at the ground without raising their head, with feet and hands tied as their soul was once tied by their greed and graspingness. The miniature carries a red flourish. (Canto XIX, v. 70-72.)

Right: The Greedy (or Avid of power) and the Prodigal. Hugh Capet presents himself to Dante; he was founder of the dynasty that reigned in France at the time when the Poet lived. The first of the Capets accused Philip III and Charles d'Anjou of prevarication. The king predicts a darker future still under Charles II of Anjou, Charles de Valois and Philip the Handsome, who becomes guilty of outrage against the vicar of Christ in Agnagni, where Guillaume de Nogaret and Sciarra Colonna, his envoys, arrested and insulted Boniface VIII. (Canto XX, v. 34-96.)

the Angel is now urging them towards the next cornice, where are the Greedy and the Prodigal. They all lie on their stomachs, bound hand and foot. The Poet questions one of them, Pope Adrian V, who, in the course of a short pontificate (hardly a month), managed to indulge in his own greed. For not having looked towards Heaven during his life, he is now forced to remain face down until his sins are forgiven.

A little further, a shade recalls in a loud voice lessons of poverty and humility: Mary, who gave birth to her child in a stable; the consul Fabricius, who refused the gifts of the Samnites and of Pyrrhus; Saint Nicolas, who saved three young maidens from dishonor by discreetly endowing them. The speaker is none other than Hugh Capet, who then tells of the founding and the history of his house, whose glory has been smeared by so much villainy.

The mountain quakes and Dante is afraid. A shade reassures him that this happens every time a soul leaves Purgatory for Heaven. The man turns out to be Statius, the Latin poet, who regrets never having known Virgil, whom he considers to be his master. Dante smiles and tells him who his guide is. Overcome with joy, Statius attempts to kiss his knees, but forgets that this earthly gesture is impossible.

76

come sono stati philippi euangi
peru nouellante franca crtta
il nuolo fur ormo boccato dipingi
quanto lirogi antichi uener meno
tutti fuor chiuno redutto imparm bigi

rouam stretto nelle manu ilfreno
del gouerno depatmo et anta rossa

The Gluttons. The three Poets—Statius has joined Dante and Virgil—go on their way and soon come to a tree which is unusual in that it tapers at the base. In addition, it bears apples which have a sweet fragrance and a fountain waters it. The artist has simplified this vision by representing an ordinary tree with rounded leaves, laden with fruit. Dante, Virgil and Statius observe this strange phenomenon and the whole scene takes on a dream quality. (Canto XXII, v. 130-141.)

Below: Forese Donati. The three Poets meet a group of Gluttons among whom Dante recognizes his friend Forese Donati by the sound of his voice. The unfortunate explains that his sad condition is due to his unquenched desire—which all souls in torment feel— to taste the fruit of the tree and the fresh water which flows abundantly. The Poets and the damned are arranged symmetrically. (Canto XXIII, v. 37-60.)

The time has now come to make their way to the Sixth Cornice. Statius accompanies his new friends. Suddenly, a magnificent tree rises before them. It is laden with delicious fruit and fed by clear water from a spring at the top of a cliff. A voice sings the praises of temperance, while they cross the place where Gluttons are kept, tempted by the view of water and fruit. An emaciated shade stops Dante. It is his friend Foresse Donati, who loses no time in inveighing against the women of Florence, accusing them of licentiousness. But Dante reminds him that they themselves were not without blame in their youth, even though his voyage

The Fornicators. On an arid and rocky slope of the mountain, the souls of fornicators guilty of lechery are purified by the flames which leap out in a way similar to that of volcanoes. The Poets make their way along a precipitous path. (Canto XXV, v. 109-117.)

Urged by Virgil, Dante overcomes his fears and follows his guide into the flames; Statius follows him. (Canto XXVII, v. 46-63.)

Following pages: The entrance to the Divine Forest, This is a large miniature in which the artist has sought to give life to the vegetation by painting a series of trees with straight trunks and rounded leaves as well as a living carpet of flowers. On one side, Virgil and Statius; on the other Dante, Lethe, and, beyond the river of Hell, Matilda picking flowers. The peacefulness of this scene is reminiscent of the Lombard miniaturists of "Tacuina Sanitatis". (Canto XXVIII, v. 1-21.)

Beatrice appears to Dante in the earthly Paradise. On a carriage drawn by a gryphon, she speaks to Dante, who is on the other bank of Lethe, reproaching him, but letting the affection she bears for him carry through. (Canto XXXI, v. 55-81.)

Right: The earthly Paradise, Dante's purification. Dante falls down under the weight of Beatrice's reproaches (first scene, left). Matilda, the beautiful woman he has met at the entrance of the earthly Paradise, throws him into Lethe, dragging him along for a certain distance before taking him out to show Beatrice to him again. (Here, the artist has simplified the scene: Beatrice herself pulls him out of the river.) Dante is now purified. He still has to perfect this purification before going to Heaven. (Canto XXXI, v. 88-104.)

through Hell and Purgatory will open the gates of Paradise, where Beatrice is waiting for him. He presents Statius to his friend; the poet is now ready to leave for Heaven, as the ritual rumbling of the mountain announces.

Still escorted by Statius, who explains how the dead become shades, Dante and Virgil arrive at the Seventh and last Cornice, where sinners of the Flesh are kept, surrounded by tongues of fire which leap out right to the edge of the cliff. Like the penitents of the other cornices, the Lechers are condemned to recite examples that refer to their sin and to its opposite, the virtue of chastity. This is the case of Guido Guinizelli, the founder of the "Dolce stil nuovo" school who tells Dante (who was the toast of the school's dining club) why he is here: he managed to repent, late in the day but sincerely, as he was about to die. But Dante hardly listens, so great is his admiration for the man, and if it were not for the flames, he would embrace him.

The pilgrim nevertheless has to expose himself to the fire to get to the top of the mountain, where Paradise is. He is not very keen on this idea and has to be encouraged by an Angel and then by Virgil. He has to be reminded that there is no other way of reaching Beatrice.

Finally, with Statius and Virgil on either side, he walks through the flames. Although the trial is short, he suffers so much that he nearly faints. He eventually finds himself standing at the foot of a long, straight staircase which leads to the great wood of the earthly Paradise. Here, Virgil tells him, you will find the joy that mortals seek in vain on earth. The moment has come for the dead Poet to leave his disciple, now that he knows the way he must follow and that he is his own master and no longer needs a guide.

All three move among the trees near a little clear-water river. Dante stops and sees on the other bank a lonely woman picking flowers. It is Matilda. She turns to him smiling and describes to the newcomers the things that grow in the earthly Paradise. Plants unknown on earth grow there and two rivers water it: Lethe, which can wipe out the memory of sin, and Eunoae, which rekindles the memory of good. A mystical procession of men and women passes near, singing the Hosanna; there is a magnificent chariot pulled by a gryphon. When it arrives in front of the Poet, the carriage stops. Surrounded by a cloud of flowers, her hair hidden by a white veil and dressed in a gown of flame red, Beatrice appears. Wanting Virgil to share his immense joy, Dante turns round, but the master is gone, and the prior of Florence breaks into tears. The young woman upbraids him for his sorrow. Only regret for his dissipated youth should bring forth such tears; it was then that he preferred false images to the perfecting of his mind. This is why she obtained Heaven's permission to make him see the suffering of Hell and Purgatory. To enter Paradise, he must yet repent. Dante, confused and torn by remorse, is overcome by Beatrice's gaze and falls swooning at her feet. He

Dante completes his purification. Reproaches to the corrupt church. The scene is divided into two episodes. In both, Beatrice is surrounded by seven nymphs who incarnate the four Cardinal Virtues and the three Theological Virtues. In the first episode, the Poet's Egeria is represented in majesty; in the second, she explains to Dante the disdain that the present state of the Church brings on in her. Eunoae is near, where Matilda (absent in this scene) will lead him on Beatrice's order and make him "pure and ready to climb to the stars". (Canto XXXIII, v. 1-78.)

awakes in Lethe, held up by Matilda. On the other bank, his smiling lady awaits him. Without taking his eyes off her face, Dante joins the procession, which sets off again singing angelic songs.

Purified by the waters of Eunoae, which bring back to him the good deeds he has accomplished, Dante is now prepared: nothing can prevent him from climbing to the stars...

Paradise

So that he can properly describe the kingdom of the Chosen, Dante calls on the help of Apollo, the god of poetry. Then, straing intently at Beatrice's face, he feels himself carried up to Heaven at a tremendous speed. At the same time, he hears the voice of the one he loves telling him that his ascension is due to the purification to which he agreed. As they arrive in the first Heaven, that of the Moon, a brilliant cloud envelopes them. Dante, who is curious about everything, wants to know what really causes the spots on the moon. The difference in splendor of the heavenly bodies, Beatrice tells him, is due to the virtue of the supreme Intelligence. It is this virtue which decides on the sharing out of light and dark. When she stops speaking, the souls that live in this Heaven show themselves. They belong to mortals who failed in their vows of chastity. Thus the Poet finds Piccarda Donati. She justifies her fault by telling him how her brother Corso forced her to leave the convent to marry Rossellino della Tosa. Thus the same fate befell her as Constance, the mother of Frederick II, who is in Heaven with her. However, the light which radiates from Constance is weaker than that which emanates from Beatrice, but Dante forebears from asking his true love questions. But as she can read his mind, she reminds him of the Platonic theory of the return of souls to the stars and the place assigned to the blessed who depending on their degree of receptivity enjoy the divine influx more or less intensely. At the speed of lightning, they move to the second Heaven, that of Mercury, where live the souls of those who tried to acquire honor and glory by doing good. More than a thousand souls radiating happiness come dancing to meet them. One of them is more than happy that a living being has reached Heaven. This is the emperor Justinian, who wears a shining halo. He tells the story of his life to the Poet, and how, with the help of the Holy Ghost, he managed to enact his famous laws. He then tells the history of the Roman Eagle from Aenaeus to the time of Dante, stressing the wrongs that the Guelphs and Ghibellines have done. When his tale is told, he rejoins the dancing choir. While Dante is hesitating to question Beatrice again, she reveals to him that mercy and divine justice are man's only salvation and that the incarnation of the Lord in Jesus Christ is the only way of redeeming man.

While they talk, they climb to the Heaven of Venus, where live the souls who loved intensely during their lives. To the accompaniment of a hosanna of infinite sweetness, Charles Martel, the Poet's friend, comes to him. An untimely death prevented this prince, son of Charles II of Anjou, from reigning over Provence and Naples, which he would certainly have governed with more wisdom than his brother Robert to whom the kingdoms were given. How, Dante asks himself, can good parents give birth to children ruled by evil? Read-

S io auessi lettor piu lungo spacio
da scriuere io piu cantarei imparte
lo dolce ber che mai non maria sacio

Ma peche pien son tutte le carte
ordite aquesta cantica seconda
non lascia piu ire lo fren delarte

Io ritornai dalla santissima onda
rifatto sicome piante nouelle
rinouellate dinouella fronda

Puro edisposto asalir alle stelle.

Qui finisce la seconda cantica della comedia
dante aligieri nella quale tratta del pur
gatorio e delanima.

La gloria di colui che tutto muoue
per luniuerso penetra erisplende
in una parte piu emeno altroue

Nel ciel che piu della sua luce prende
fu io e uidi cose che ridire
ne sa ne puo chi dilla su discende

Pero che apressando se al suo disire
nostro intelletto si profonda tanto
che dietro la memoria non puo ire

Veramente quanto del regno santo
nella mia mente potei far tesoro
sara ora materia del mio canto

Buono appollo alultimo lauoro
fame del tuo ualore si fatto uaso
come dimandi dar lamato alloro

Infino aqui lun giogo di parnaso
assai mi fu ma or con ambedue
me uopo entrar nellaringo rimaso

Entra nel petto mio espira tue
sicome quando marsia traesti
della guaina delle membra sue

O diuina uirtu se mi ti presti
tanto che lombra del beato regno
segnato nel mio capo io manifesti

Vederai al pie del tuo diletto legno
uenire e coronarmi delle foglie
che lla materia e tu mi farai degno

Si rade uolte padre sene coglie
per triumphar o cesaro o poeta
colpa o uergogna delle humane uoglie

Che partorir letitia en sulla lieta
delphica deita dourria la fronda
penea quando alcun di se asseta

Poca fauilla gran fiamma seconda
forse dirietro ame con miglior uoci
si preghera perche cirra risponda

Surge amortali per diuerse foci
la lucerna del mondo ma da quella
che quattro cerchi gionge contre croci

Con miglior corso e con miglior stella
esce congiunta e la mondana cera
piu asuo modo tempra e suggella

Fatto auea dilla mane e coniquesta sera
cal fece quasi e caute era libiancho
quello cimispero e laltra parte nera

Quando beatrice il sul sinistro fianco
uidi riuolta en guardar nel sole
aquila si no lise afisse unquancho

Et si come secondo raggio sole
uscir del primo en sulir in suso
pur come pellegrin che tornar uole

Cosi delatto suo plioxchi infuso
nellymagine mia cinuo si fece

Ascension. Dante, believing himself to be still in the earthly Paradise, cannot understand why the light is suddenly so bright and the music so gentle. Beatrice tells him that he has ascended to the first Heaven, or Heaven of the Moon, at the speed of lightning. (Canto I, v. 82-93.)

Right: Beatrice, turned towards the Poet and holding him by the hand, takes him into Heaven of the Moon, which is the nearest to the Earth. The artist shows them after this has happened with Beatrice pointing to Heaven, inviting Dante to give thanks to God. (Canto II, v. 22-36.)

ing his thoughts, Charles replies: if good and evil were handed down unaltered from generation to generation, there would soon be an imbalance in one way or another. This is why divine Providence equally shares among men the traits of character that inspire their conduct.

It is now Cunizza da Romano who hails Dante. The sister of the infamous Ezzelino had predicted great unhappiness to the inhabitants of the Treviso Marches as well as to those of Feltre, whose bishop was guilty of high treason.

Another soul, as shining as that of Cunizza, comes towards him. It is that of Folquet de Marseille, a troubadour, who, after a life of adventure, became a monk and a bishop. He denounces the excessive interest that priest have for money, especially the florin, the currency of Florence. Were it not for the splendor of the souls around him. Dante, who was quite unaware of his latest ascent, would not realize that he has reached the Heaven of the Sun. The souls of twelve wise men and doctors of the church form a moving crown around him and Beatrice, and their songs express the perfect happiness of the blessed. One of them, Thomas of Aquinas, tells Dante that nothing could be refused to a living being that God had allowed to enter Heaven. Then he presents some of his companions: Albert the Great, Gratian, Pierre Lombard, Solomon and Severino Boethius. Radiating a blinding light, the famous theologian reads the Poet's thoughts before they are even formed. Anticipating his question, he names the two most illustrious defenders of the Church: Francis of Assisi, whose humble and saintly life he recounts, and Saint Dominic, whose code he exalts as it led him to eternal life. But the order he founded has much degenerated and few Dominicans, Thomas concludes, are worthy of the name.

Then Saint Bonaventure, a Franciscan, takes his turn to praise Saint Dominic, emphasizing his admirable preaching qualities. He points out each of the blessed who, like shining stars, sing and dance to

94

Piccarda Donati. Piccarda Donati belonged to a famous Florentine family; she was the sister of Forese and Corso Donati. She explains to Dante that, having been forced to enter a convent and never having been able to keep the vow of chastity, although against her will, she is in the lowest and least glorious Heaven.

The variety of faces and attitudes can be noted, as well as the splendor of the garments of the saints surrounding Piccarda. The scene is at the same time contained and full of movement. (Canto III, v. 34-57.)

The empress Constance. Dante's doubts. Piccarda shows Dante—who is still accompanied by Beatrice—the empress Constance, and mother of Frederick II of Swabia last of the Norman royalty who was married against her will to Henry VI of France. The moon, grossly retouched by a talentless dauber, is placed above the four characters. Here, the heavenly body symbolizes the Heaven where are united the blessed who could not by their own will keep their vows. (Canto III, v. 109-120.)

Following pages: Charles Martel, king of Hungary. We are in the Heaven of Venus, with the goddess herself carrying her scepter and escorted by the astrological sign of Libra and a young deer. She rules over loving spirits. Dante listens to the story of Charles Martel, who is surrounded by courtiers. The scene takes place in the vastness of the starry heavens and with the pomp due to a king. Charles Martel (1271-1295) was the elder son of Charles II of Anjou. He died too young to inherit either the kingdom of Provence or of Naples. Dante had met him in Florence in 1294. (Canto VIII, v. 40-84.)

uoma feuaremon fectu ripenti
come tumana carne fessi allora
bella prima parenta intrambo fensi

Bei arcori omego insu pido
chella bella aprigna insollcamee
nguise uoltn nel teico epiaclo

oscia cheliocchi miei ti foro offerti
alla mia donna reverenti cessa
fatti lauica dise conteri cecta

olscusi alaluce cieppromessa
ento sauca coistare sue chi
uocc mia vigilance affecto ipressa
canta equale unmo lei farsi piue
alegreiza noua chessa crebe
nismo incla alalcantere sue

uolge ccontenta fieffe uertute
fua prouedencia inquesti corpi grandi
non pur lentutur prouedute
sono inlumtte chedu esse pfettu
ma esse insieme colla lor salutte

Cunizza da Romano. In the Heaven of Venus. Dante, still guided by Beatrice, speaks with Cunizza da Romano, seen dressed in red and surrounded by beautiful women and many colors. It is surprising that Dante should have placed the daughter of Ezzelino da Romano in Heaven. This sensual woman had in fact three husbands and a large number of lovers, including, it is thought, the poet Sordello. The reason is probably because she converted towards the end of her life and from then on led a virtuous existence. It is not impossible that Dante sought to sing the praises of the redeeming powers of love, which, for him, was not incompatible with carnal passion. In addition, he had met Cunizza as a child. (Canto IX, v. 25-36.)

Below: Folquet de Marseille. Still in the Heaven of Venus, Folquet of Marseille, a Provençal troubadour, who became bishop of Toulouse and persecutor of the Albigensians, tells his story to Dante. (Canto IX, v. 64-108.)

Following pages: The Heaven of the Sun, or Sages. The artist has shown several episodes here: the ascension to the Heaven of the Sun, with Aries and Libra, the zodiac signs which are known for their beneficial influence on the Heavens; Dante thanking God for his mysterious ascension to the Heaven of the Sun; Saint Thomas Aquinas introducing himself (to right) and his master Albert of Cologne, then below, Graziano, Pier Lombardo, Solomon, Denys the Areopagite, Paul Orose, Severino Boezio, who all seem to be on the point of dancing. In this Areopagus where pagans, Hebrews and Christians mingle, there should be Isidore of Seville, the Venerable Bede, Richard de Saint-Victor and Siger de Brabant. (Canto X, v. 28-63 and 96-138.)

The Heaven of the Sun. Saint Bonaventure (a Franciscan) sings the praises of Saint Dominic in reply to the praises of Saint Francis by Saint Thomas (a Dominican). The first miniature shows (top) the Blessed and (bottom) Saint Bonaventure. (Canto XII, v. 46-105.)

Right: The Heaven of the Sun. Beatrice asks the Sages to dissipate Dante's doubt about the luminosity of souls after the resurrection of the body. (Canto XIV, v. 1-60.)

express their joy. Thomas of Aquinas returns to explain the perfect works of the Holy Ghost, such as the creation of Adam and the conception of the Virgin Mary. Man, he says, must never judge by appearances: only God's judgment counts.

The joy of Heaven becomes such that the Poet cries out that men would never fear death if they knew what happiness there was in Heaven. Then he asks what will become of the light of the blessed after the Last

Judgment, when souls will find their bodies again. Solomon explains that the perfection achieved by the whole being can only increase in splendor because of a total vision of God.

Shortly afterwards, Dante, whose eyes are only for Beatrice, feels himself transported upwards again. In the red Heaven of Mars, the souls fly around while singing, and form the shape of a cross at the center of which Christ shines. These are the Martyrs for the Faith and those who died fighting for it. As the shade of Anchises ran towards Aenaeus when the latter was going through the Elysian Fields, that of Cacciaguida, great-great-grandfather of Dante, runs to the Poet. Killed in the Holy Land during the Second Crusade, he was famed for his great virtue and his generous heart. But he was only like all the other Florentines whose sole care at the time was to protect the peace and the culture of their city. Encouraged by his Lady, Dante asks his ancestor what the origins of their family were, as well as for the names of the most illustrious citizens of the city. Cacciaguida tells of his life and his death, lists the noble houses which made Florence Rome's rival: "No one had reason to cry, not like today. The lily on our coat of arms did not change color according to the master of the moment."

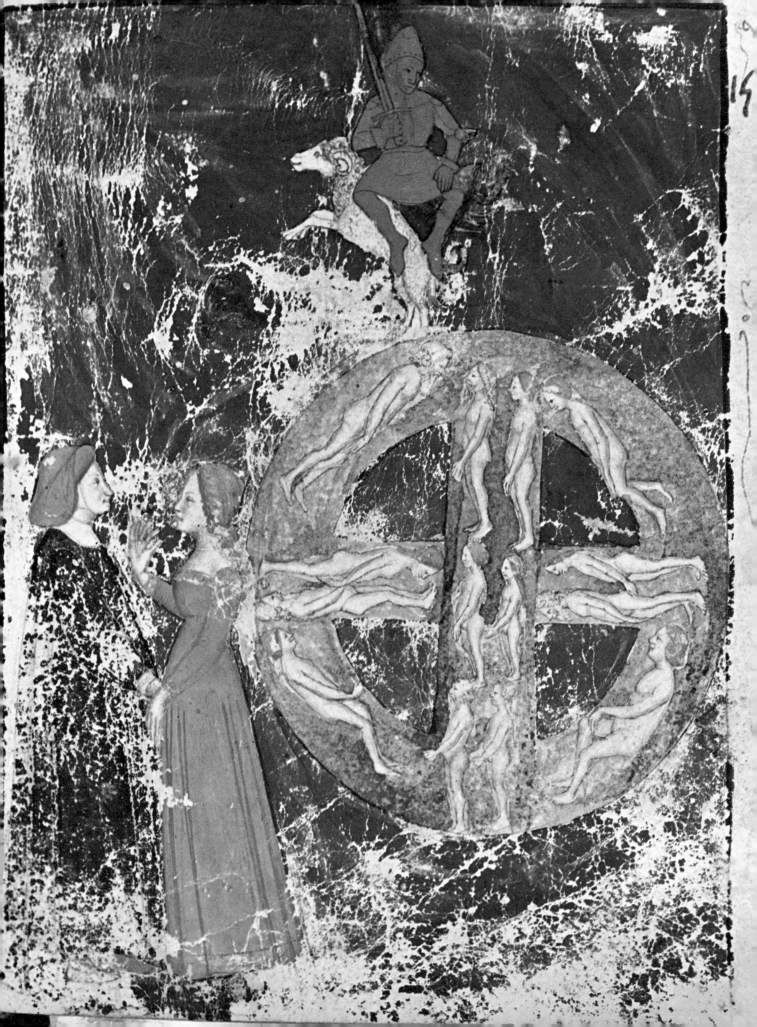

Left: The Heaven of Mars. Cacciaguida, Dante's great-great-grandfather, who died in the Holy Land, prophesies the misfortunes which await the Poet. A few famous families will, however, bring him comfort in their hospitality, such as the Scaliger of Verona, where Cangrande accepted him during his exile. His ancestor assures him that the certainty of glory will keep him going, while those who exile him will appear for what they are. (Canto XVII, v. 37-99.)

Right: The Heaven of Jupiter. The shape formed by the Just and the Pious. Taking on the aspect of imperial Roman eagles, they form a single being which speaks through the agent of some of the creatures which make up the shape. The voice of David comes from the eagle's beak. Dante is dressed in red and Beatrice in a green gown with her blond hair standing out. (Canto XX, v. 22-72.)

Left: The Heaven of Saturn or of Contemplative Spirits. An armed Saturn is placed between the lion and the unicorn. (It should be noted that in 1300, during March, Saturn was in the constellation of Leo; the unicorn was chosen by the artist to underline the cold nature of the planet.) The great staircase, which in the text rises to the Empyrean, is only shown as a modest golden ladder. Saint Peter Damian can be seen telling Dante his life story. Saints surround the ladder. (Canto XXI, v. 1-24, 25-42, 103-126.)

Above: The Heaven of Saturn. Saint Benedict carrying the mitre and the crozier telling Dante how he founded his order. On the right, a group of Benedictines. (Canto XXII, v. 97-105.)

As to his own destiny, the Poet learns a sinister prediction from the great crusader: he will have to leave his dear homeland to err from town to town and "know the taste of salt in other people's bread". But he is told not to hate his fellow citizens for this, as their villainy will be punished while he will receive eternal glory.

Looking deep into Beatrice's eyes, Dante rises to the Heaven of Jupiter, which is even brighter and bigger. The crowd of saints is spread out to form the motto: *Diligite justitiam qui judicatis terram* (Love justice, you who judge the earth). The souls, those of just and wise princes, then form to draw the image of an eagle, emblem of justice, in the sky. Dante takes the opportunity to stigmatize the greed of the clergy, which has forgotten Saint Peter and Paul, but can well remember Saint John because his head is depicted on golden florins...

The eagle then speaks to him of the impenetrable and perfect divine justice which is opposed by many Christian princes whose conduct rouses hate in peoples and ruins states. In contrast, King David, the emperors Trajan and Constantine rejoice in the sight of God as a recompense for what they have done.

Beatrice's smile now begins to fade as the Heaven of Saturn, where the couple arrive, imparts such luster to the young woman's beauty that Dante would be turned to ashes if he were only to lift his eyes to her.

Left: The Heaven of the Fixed Stars. Saint Benedict rises, as soon as he has finished speaking, to join his companions. At Beatrice's urging, Dante also goes up the golden staircase to penetrate the sign of the Twins, in which the sun stood when he was born. (Canto XXII, v. 22-51.)

Right: Supplication to the constellation of the Twins. Dante, who remembers that he was born under this sign, to which he attributes his genius, addresses a fervent prayer to it to give him the strength to describe his vision. The Twins, naked like athletes and side by side, are shown here in a blue sky the shape of a semi-circle, which is covered with tongues of flame. Beatrice standing, and Dante kneeling, pray near a mountain slope. (Canto XXII, v. 112-123.)

Above: The Triumph of Christ and Mary. The triumph of Christ and Mary, the apparition of all the saints, the indescribable beauty of Mary crowned by the light of an angel, the return of the whole heavenly court to the Empyrean, finally the soft hymn that the Chosen sing for Mary: all this has been condensed by the artist into one illustration, and is reminiscent of an altar piece where Jesus and Mary are seen on a throne. The angel presents a crown which Jesus puts on his mother's head; beside it and above, the musician angels; immediately below, the twelve apostles, near whom the artist has drawn a preceding event: Beatrice shows Dante the zenith where the miracle of the two triumphs will appear. The miniature summarizes the whole of Canto XXIII. (Canto XXIII, v. 1-139.)

Right: Dante examined on Faith. Beatrice presents Dante to Saint Peter for his examination on Faith. The Poet replies so well with theological doctrine that the Master embraces him. (Canto XXIV, v. 1-54.)

This is the Heaven of the Meditators. They climb up and down a golden staircase around which they dance together, afterwards looking like globes of fire. One of them, Pier Damiano, who, on becoming cardinal retreated to a humble monastery cell, tells his life story to the Poet, insisting that the cardinal's hat was too great a weight for him to bear, while several prelates, Dante's contemporaries, think only of luxury and their weel-being. A great clamor then arises to announce the appearance of a sparkling whirlwind which carries

The starry Heaven. Saint Peter complains of his successors. On the blue background crossed by golden rays, Dante and Beatrice can be seen one behind the other, turned towards Saint Peter, who is followed by Adam, Saint James and Saint John the Baptist: all listen attentively as Saint Peter complains bitterly about the corrupt popes who have followed him. (Canto XXVII, v. 10-27.)

A point that is God. According to the text of the Divine Comedy, the Poet sees a point of immobile light in the sky, whose glow he cannot resist. Around the point are nine luminous circles which are near to the center of this huge sphere. These are the nine choirs of angels. The artist has painted the scene with a circle of uneven red—the color becomes gradually brighter towards the center, where he has painted the face of Christ with blond hair and a twin-pointed beard. Angels turn all around in the most diverse positions. Below, Dante and Beatrice in adoration in a square of sky. (Canto XXVIII, v. 13-45.)

Above: The Creation of the angels. Beatrice tells Dante how the angels were created and tries to clear up his wrong impressions on the subject. As he could not illustrate these points of doctrine, the artist has represented God in majesty. Angels are on each side, and on the left is Dante, to whom Beatrice explains the theological mystery. As a background to the Almighty's throne, a Romanesque construction in which Gothic influences can be detected. The upper part looks rather like the Castel Sant'Angelo in Rome (Canto XXIX, v. 31-69.)

Right: The glory of Mary. The triumph of Mary on her throne, surrounded by musician angels. Below, the saints in ecstasy pray while looking at the Virgin. Among the various religious orders and mitred clergy (bishops and patriarchs), Saint Bernard can be seen taking Beatrice's place beside Dante. He intercedes in the Poet's favor so that he can obtain a vision of Mary and the of God. (Canto XXXI, v. 118-142.)

116

Below right, Dante, kneeling in front of Saint Bernard, obtains the right to see Mary in majesty. The artist has again drawn an altar piece, with Mary sitting on a marble throne of Gothic inspiration. Around her are characters from the Old and New Testaments, as well as the Archangel Gabriel, who offers her a bouquet of lilies. Mary holds her right hand to her heart as a sign of love and carries a sacred book in her lap. (Canto XXXII.)

the beatified souls of great men. Saint Benedict, the founder of the Monte Cassino monastery and of the order which works for the glory of the Church, leaves it and comes to Dante. He deplores the corruption of monks, who, instead of thinking of the poor, spend much of their time appropriating church property.

At a sign from Beatrice, Dante quickly climbs the staircase which leads to the Heaven of Fixed Stars. He finds himself in the constellation of the Twins, the sign under which he was born and to which he believes he owes his genius. He asks the constellation to help him describe the magnificence of the view that is his: the seven Heavens that he has crossed and, far away, the earth, where, unfortunately, men continue to fight and hate each other. And this thought inspires a deep pity in him.

Beatrice, to whom the Poet has turned, invites him to admire the blessed who are celebrating the triumph of Christ. His emotion is so great that he cannot describe it. The saintly smile of his lady fills him with intense happiness. But now she shows him an even more radiant sight: that of the heavenly choir surrounding the Virgin and the Apostles, themselves lit up by the light of Christ.

The souls surround the couple like a burning crown, then, fascinated by the power of divine love that

The Empyrean. This miniature is not very different from the previous one. Here, however, Mary is placed beside Jesus on a great throne. Musician angels surround this vision, while the lower part represents the apostles and the saints. Amond the saints of lower order are Saint Peter and Paul, then the other apostles. More to the right, Saint Bernard pleads with the Virgin to let Dante enjoy the vision of God. The saint cannot be seen very well because of the poor state of conservation of the miniature. Note the delicacy of touch in the painting of the musician angels. (Canto XXXIII, v. 1-39.)

120

io chalhne oicuci oiui
apropinquaua sicboimo oouca
lardoroo oel oisioeno mme sinu
B ernaroo maceraua esoroea
p cbio guaroasse suso maio era
gia p me stesso tal qualei uolea

emanates from Beatrice, Saint Peter, the guardian of Paradise, comes down to them. He asks the Poet several questions about faith and, satisfied with his answers, blesses him. But Dante still has to present himself to Saint James and Saint John. The first asks him about Hope, which the Florentine answers is "the certain expectation of the glory to come", a virtue inspired by the reading of sacred texts and by the Epistles written by his examiner. Saint John asks Dante to speak to him of Charity. The traveler sees it as feeling of love that man has for God that is dictated to him by philosophical reasoning and by the absolute perfection of the Creator.

At these words the whole of Paradise starts to sing the hymn "Glory to the Father, to the Son and to the Holy Ghost", while Adam, the first man, joins the apostles Peter, James and John. The first pope tells of the shame he feels at the spread of corruption in which so many of his successors wallow without shame. The time will come, praised be the Lord, when divine Providence will save the Church.

Carried once again by the irresistible gaze of his Lady, Dante climbs to the Crystalline Heaven or First Mobile. Here the angelic hierarchies are spread in nine concentric circles and spin like spheres of fire around God. Beatrice tells her companion of the creation of the angels and their essence, of the fall of Lucifer and of the privilege given to those who always faced God and were multiplied to infinity.

In the Empyrean, the supreme Heaven of Paradise, a river of light welcomes the Poet. Like sparks, angels land on the flowers which cover it, before diving into the resplendent wave of souls. But as soon as Dante leans towards the blinding flood it changes into a circle around which appears the Rose, each petal of which is the throne of a saint. At its heart, to which Beatrice leads him, Dante inhales the ineffable fragrance that it exudes. In this glory, the Poet sees only the faces radiated by divine grace and he closely observes everything so that he can describe it on his return to earth. But suddenly, Beatrice disappears. An old man takes her place and he smiles benevolently at Dante. "She is there, he tells him, at the third degree of the Rose." The old man is none other than Saint Bernard, who invites Dante to make his preparations to meet God. After having warned the Poet that he must obtain the intercession of the Virgin before he can do this, the founder of the Cistercian order turns to Mary, who is at the summit of the Rose. The indescribable beatitude of the Mother of Jesus fills the saints who surround her with supreme joy. "O Virgin, Mother and Daughter of your Son", Bernard begins, while Dante stares intensely at the one who gave birth to Christ.

With a sign of her head, the Virgin accepts the Saint's supplications and turns her eyes towards the Almighty as if to incite Dante to imitate her. The Poet's gaze penetrates into the light of God and loses itself in it. He sees the truth in a flash, by divine grace, but he can go no further as his strength fails him.

From then on, everything in him conforms to the "Love which moves the sun and the stars".

Designed and produced by
Productions Liber SA

© Productions Liber SA
and Éditions Minerva SA
Fribourg - Genève, 1979

Printed by
Printer Industria Gráfica SA
Barcelone, Espagne
Depósito legal : B. 23110-1979
Printed in Spain

First English edition published by Productions Liber S.A.
and Editions Minerva S.A., Fribourg - Genève.

Library of Congress Catalog
Card Number PQ4329-D3 851,1 79-14588

I.S.B.N. 0-517-28287-9

This edition is distributed by Crescent Books,
a division of Crown Publishers, Inc.

a b c d e f g h